I'm

Still

Here

After All I've Been Through...

I'm

Still

With A Praise.

Dr. Yvonne Capehart

YC Publishing Company
Pensacola, FL

Published by
YC Publications
P.O. Box 15597
Pensacola, FL 32514

Cover design and book production by
SHARE Design Studio
3020 W. Brainerd St.
Pensacola, FL 32505

Foreword

*E*veryone has things in their past that tries to reach into the present and hamper their spiritual walk. Broken relationships, unforgiveness, traumatic childhood or young adult episodes, and many other things can open the door to spiritual hindrances. The enemy of our soul uses these things like a ball and chain to hold us back from the purpose God has ordained for each of us. In her new book, "I'm Still Here", Dr. Yvonne Capehart addresses this issue from a personal and scriptural standpoint.

Dr. Capehart bares her heart as she writes of experiences in her past that kept her from fulfilling God's call on her life. As you read this book you will no doubt see similarities in your own life. You will learn that the thing keeping you from your destiny may have roots in your past.

Dr. Capehart uses her personal experiences and God's Word to point us to the path of victory over these strongholds birthed in our past. She teaches us to move beyond our hurts and push forward into the place where God wants us to be. Dr. Capehart is not only "Still Here"; she is a powerful voice for God bringing his Word to the wounded and hurt.

My prayer is that as you read, "I'm Still Here" you will allow God's Spirit to begin a work of deliverance in your life and that once delivered you will step into the purpose to which God has called you. Having done this, we can say as Paul said, "...*forgetting those things which are behind, and reaching forth unto those things which are before, I press toward the mark for the prize of the high calling of God in Christ Jesus.*"

Co-Pastor Darlene Bishop

Dedication

*T*his book is dedicated to the many women who refuse to be hindered from reaching their purpose. You may have experienced an abundance of trials which have come to stop you from reaching your destiny. You may have gone through more than you thought you could ever go through, but you went through. The enemy may have stolen some material things, robbed you of some friends, and put you in some uncomfortable situations for a season. However, he could not take your peace, and he could not stop your praise. I pray that God gives you the boldness to stand up and to proclaim to the world, After all I have been through, I'm Still Here, with a praise. I hope this book provokes you to your purpose.

Acknowledgments

*F*irst and foremost, thank you Lord for your grace and mercy and for the strength to allow my problems to provoke me to my purpose and despite what I have been through, I'm still here, delivered with destiny.

To my husband, Lee, who demonstrates the true meaning of love. Your love gave me the strength to reach my destiny and the courage to stand once I got there. You have always encouraged me to go beyond what I see. Thank you for allowing me to obey the call of God on my life.

To my sons, Brandon and Britton, who are expressions of God's greatest gift to me. Thanks for being great guys. To Chauncey Rease, thanks for all you do. You are more of a blessing in my life than you will ever know.

To my mother, Earnestine Chandler McKinnon, and my family, for your never ending love, support and your understanding of the call of God on my life. Mother, you guided me in the right direction; thanks for a wonderful family.

To Tammy Whiten, Lateece Kyles and Carolyn Key you are the greatest armorbearers one could have; thanks for your patience, support, understanding, and encouragement. Most of all, thanks for holding up my arms, especially when it seemed my strength was failing. Your labor is not in vain.

To the Sister Keeper staff and representatives across the country, thanks for pushing me to my purpose and for your support.

To John Hoskins thank you for the editorial assistance, God will reward you richly.

To my church family at Believers' Life Center, thank you for the hours of intercessory prayer and for your support. Thank you all for pushing me to my destiny. I pray that you will receive a prophet's reward.

Contents

Introduction

*D*o you feel that you have had to endure more pain than you could bare? Have you gone through too much to go on? Do you feel that the value of your anointing is over-priced compared to the cost of your struggle? Are you constantly finding yourself stepping out of one hole, only to step into another?

It is through the making and breaking process of spiritual struggles that strength is released, and death to self brings deliverance. We must push past our problems and into our purpose. We have focused on the struggles long enough. We should focus on "where do I go from here?" It is time for believers to go through their situations, their pitfalls and their struggles by allowing their "problems to provoke them to their purpose," and to walk in the authority of the Holy Spirit that God has given them.

We must cease whining and complaining about the things going wrong in life. Sorrow over our situations should quickly turn to praise when we see others who have fallen into our same dilemmas but were unable to break free from the web of the enemy. Some chose death; others ran away; some decided to stay, but are full of hate. Nonetheless, you who stayed in the fight and have made it through your situations, you are ***Still Here With A Praise***.

"And we know that all things work together for good to them that love God, to them who are the called according to his purpose" (Romans 8:28). Are you called by God? If your answer is "yes," ***I'm Still Here*** will bring comfort and understanding, and inspire you to finally realize that you have been divinely predestined to reach your purpose. My friend, you must accept the fact that God's plan and purpose is for you to reach your destiny in Him, knowing you have been "called to conquer and chosen to change" this generation.

Do not allow the jerks and sudden swirls of the ever-turning Potter's wheel to give you motion-sickness, but use each turn to advance to the next level of promotion. It doesn't matter how many times you are thrown into the fiery furnace, nor the temperature of the heat. Just know that God is there with you.

When the enemy comes back expecting to find you dead, and expecting to prepare for your funeral, he should run in defeat when he sees you still standing, boldly proclaiming: "I'm not dead, depressed, or confused—and I'm not giving up! I may have gone through some things that tried to take my life, but ***I'm Still Here***".

Chapter One

~Discovering a L. U. M. P. ~
Leaving Unwanted Memories in the Past

*W*hile I was driving home early one morning, the Lord commanded me to tell women to discover the lumps. Instinctively I thought, "does someone close to me have breast cancer?" Breast cancer is one of the leading causes of death among women. You may have a friend, coworker, or loved one who is struggling with the horrors of this disease. Although this terrible illness has taken the life of many, early detection has preserved thousands of other lives.

I soon realized that God wanted the women to discover the spiritual lumps in their lives. The mere thought of finding a lump in your breast is quite dreadful. The pain, shame, and embarrassment of the possible outcome after discovering a lump in their breast, cause some women to deny their reality. Some convince themselves that it only hurts if they touch it; therefore, they avoid touching the area as much as possible. Many women act as if the day of discovery never happened.

"Brethren, I count not myself to have apprehended: but this one thing I do, forgetting those things which are behind, and reaching forth unto those things which are before."
—Philippians 3:13

1

However, letting the lump grow and fester can allow it to transform into an even greater monster: cancer. We cannot afford to go into denial. Denial could mean death.

What are the spiritual lumps no woman wants to discover? What spiritual lumps, if left unattended, will grow to contaminate the entire body? These lumps could be feelings of rejection after divorce, the loss of a loved one, intimidation, unresolved pain, rejection, abuse, unforgiveness, and even failures, if not confronted and given closure. Spiritual lumps can also represent areas of weakness, or past mistakes. God wants you to realize that these things have caused a lump to appear in your spirit. **1 John 1:9** says, *"If we confess our sins, he is faithful and just to forgive us our sins, and to cleanse us from all unrighteousness."*

Are there areas in your life that cause you pain if touched? Does the thought of finding a lump bring fear to your soul? Can you remember when you discovered a lump in your spirit and the singe of pain that flowed throughout your body each time you were forced to touch that area? Are you mentally tormented by the notion that the discovery of a lump could cost you your destiny or even your life? All too often, this is where the battle begins for many women. Before many of them seek help for issues that have invaded their spirit and become rooted in their soul, they first battle with admitting there is a lump there at all. Often they say, "I know I felt something, but it could have been my imagination," or "I'll check next month to see if it's still there." Subsequently, when the next month comes, they are too preoccupied with the discovery of a second lump to deal with the first.

Extracting a L.U.M.P.

"For though we walk in the flesh, we do not war after the flesh; For the weapons of our warfare are not carnal, but mighty through God to the pulling down of strong holds. Casting down imaginations, and every high thing that exalteth itself against the knowledge of God, and bringing into captivity every thought to the obedience of Christ."

--2 Corinthians 10: 3-5

Discovering a lump in your life is the easy part. Admitting that you must deal with the situation is another issue. You must bind every stronghold hindering you from gaining complete deliverance. During this stage of my own deliverance, the Lord showed me the unclean spirits that had entered my life as a child through negative comments, rejections, and many other strongholds. God led me through a process of spiritual warfare against the stronghold of rejection and all the strongholds that surrounded my family, myself, and my environment.

One of the more serious strongholds I discovered in my life was the emptiness I felt growing up without a father. I had a wonderful loving mother who worked endlessly to provide all that she could for the family. Although God provided and sent miracles after miracles for our family, the feelings of emptiness remained in my heart.

3

One of the most disturbing memories of feeling unloved was at age eleven when I saw my father for the first time after a seven-year absence. We were sitting around the table eating breakfast when my father walked in. His introduction began with his attempting to identify each of us by name. He went from the eldest to the youngest. However, when he came to me, the next to the youngest child, he could not remember my name. He struggled for a moment and appeared to draw a blank. My older sister said, "Daddy, that's Yvonne."

Allowing that moment to have such an impact on my life seems senseless now, but the pain of that memory haunted me until my adult life. It was not enough that he had rejected to love me as his daughter; but he magnified the rejection by forgetting my name. I brushed it off as nothing and denied that I felt a lump in my spirit each time I touched that area of my life. The stronghold of rejection began to infect my entire soul.

I longed to understand why my father did not love us enough to stay and be a "daddy." Although I felt a vast emptiness, I became good at making others believe I was "full." As life went on, I tucked the pain away, and never talked about it to anyone. Discussing it made me admit that I was hurting, and caused me to deal with the pain. There was no way I was about to admit I was hurting for the love of someone who had rejected me. Despite my pain, I continued praying and longing for the day when my father would embrace me and love me as his daughter. No matter how I tried to disguise my anguish behind a mask of self-deception, God knew that beneath it all was a heart filled with secret hurt and shame.

Rejection led to the development of many dark childhood secrets, and several adult pitfalls. Each level of rejection brought about a different mask. I too, forgot who I was. I felt I needed a male figure to validate my existence. It wasn't until later in my life, after being married for a few years to a wonderful man, that I discovered my lump of emptiness and the rejection had grown into an even greater problem. The feelings of rejection made me insecure in the way I received love, as well as the way I shared it. I blamed my sudden emotional outbursts on everything from the house not being cleaned, to being overworked, to other people, or everything but the right thing. A simple hug from my spouse was a major task for me to embrace. Once I discovered the lumps in my past, it was revealed to me that I had buried an incident from my childhood that caused me to resist being affectionate to others. Thank God for deliverance, and for a loving husband.

We may not be able to hide the physical scars of our past; but we have mastered the art of concealing emotional wounds buried deep within. To our friends and co-workers we seem fine, while our husbands, children, and loved ones are compelled to watch hopelessly as our lives slowly crumble from the pain of hidden shame.

Spiritual lumps can contaminate the healthy areas of your life. They can stop you from accepting a promotion for which you know you are more than qualified. Lumps can cause you to hate the man of your dreams who you know loves you more than life itself. Lumps will cause you to bury your dreams and abort your seed.

We are informed by doctors to examine our breasts and bodies each month for any signs of foreign masses. Early detection means longer life. My friends, God wants us to constantly examine our lives for foreign masses that come only to hinder us from reaching our potential in Christ. At the first sign of discovery, go to God, the master surgeon, and allow Him to quickly remove unwanted forces from your life.

It takes the touch of a specialist who is qualified to put you to sleep, one who can put you in a position that gives Him complete control, in order to bring change to your life. While lying before Him in the operating room, allow Him to convince you to release total trust to the master surgeon, and to assure you that when you get up, it will all be over.

Sometimes admitting that the lump is there may bring an even greater sense of discomfort at that moment but it will ease. During the extraction process you may experience discomfort from the cutting, pain from the removal, and even some bleeding from the loss. However, the recovery process brings hope for a new life with a new beginning. **Psalms 30:5** says, *" Weeping may endure for a night, but joy cometh in the morning."*

For the success and future of my family I knew I had to discard the lumps of my soul, and to allow God to completely heal me. God finally got my attention and instructed me to admit that there was a painful area in my life. He allowed me to cry and express all the hurt, pain, and shame I felt.

After pouring out my feelings to God, He said, "It happened and there is nothing you can do to change it. Are you willing to allow it to destroy your life and who you are?" God instructed me to never cry over this situation again. He began to take me through a healing process that changed my life forever. He led me to forgive my father whether he ever accepted me or not. I had to release him in order to free myself.

Psalms 147:3 reads, *"He healeth the broken in heart and bindeth up their wounds."* The broken hearted are those who are deeply distressed and in trouble of any kind. **Proverbs 15:13** says, *"But by sorrow of the heart, the spirit is broken."* As long as you or your heart is in sorrow, your spirit will be broken.

Past sin is another area from which we must gain release. There were many sinful acts in which I found myself involved. Even after I had been delivered from the hand of the enemy, I felt trapped by the bondage of shame. David says in **Psalms 41:4**, *"Lord be merciful unto me, heal my soul, for I have sinned against thee."* Problems, troubles, and sins are some of the things that can wound our soul and hinder us from achieving our total deliverance in God. Acknowledging past memories of abuse and mistakes can be very painful; however, being delivered from them can be even more painful. During the cancer treatment many patients undergo chemotherapy. The strain of chemotherapy may cause fatigue, nausea, and even hair loss. Likewise, you may have to lose something in your cleansing process; but the results will bring healing to your soul and peace to your life.

I was forced to face the sin in my life. Every time I fell into sin, I would brush it off as simply having a bad day. Soon, one bad day lead to a bad week, and then to a bad month. I had a problem. Eventually, I could no longer brush the problem off; it had grown too big for me to push away.

I was going to church day after day, night after night, to revivals, conferences, and virtually anywhere, continually searching for some anointed person to free me from the torment within. I would be called up to the altar and given a powerful word about what God was going to do in my life, and how He was going to use me one day. Nevertheless, I needed help "today!" I would quickly doubt the genuineness of the men and women of God. I would leave thinking: "if they were really prophets why didn't they see the sin in my life?" Perhaps they did.

I eventually fell deeper into the pit of hell than I thought I ever would. Still, I knew God! I knew He loved me. I knew He didn't want me bound and shackled by the sin and torment in my life. The things that once held me hostage seem so insignificant today. Perhaps they came to make me strong.

I will never forget the day I turned to Him. I told Him that I wanted to be totally set free: free to smile, free to laugh, and free to just live. I wanted peace in my mind. I needed to be able to come into His presence and not be ashamed.

What God instructed me to do was beyond my expectation, but I obeyed him. I had nothing to lose and everything to gain. He told me that my deliverance was going to come through me.

I had invited unclean spirits to abide in my home, heart, and life. I now had to command them to leave. I went into my bathroom and began to command every unclean spirit to loose me, in the name of Jesus. I felt the strongholds break off of my life. When I came out, I knew that I had been totally changed.

I fought to tear down the walls I had built to protect my heart and soul from ever having to experience the pain of rejection. We must realize that there are going to be moments in life when people are not going to understand who we are, nor understand our purpose. We must quickly forgive and move forward. I had to forgive everyone and every incident that had ever happened to me.

You too must forgive those who have mistreated you, as well as forgive yourself. Unforgiveness will eat at your soul worse than cancer. People may have hurt you, and may never want to talk to you again; but you must forgive them. Another thing just dropped in my spirit that I feel compelled to include for some precious reader. You may not have the opportunity to hold the child in your hands that you aborted because of fear,shame, or your inability to care for the child. Nonetheless, you cannot change the past. Forgive yourself and live! You must forgive your father or loved one who molested, raped, or mentally abused you. You must also forgive your spouse for abandoning you. Stop a moment and take a personal inventory. Are there unresolved issues waiting on your forgiveness? If so, do it now.

After admitting that I needed to be healed and delivered, my life began to change. Once God took me through the healing and forgiving process, I was able to uproot and release the spirit of rejection out of the core of my own spirit. God later revealed to me that lumps cannot be forgotten until they have been discovered and discarded. God said, "L.U.M.P. simply means to Leave Unwanted Memories in the Past." In order to leave them in the past, we must be healed and released from them. Lumps outside of the body are harmless. Once they have been removed from your spirit, they are ineffective in invading your soul.

I was now able to experience something I had never experienced in my life: the love, guidance, correction, and most of all, safety of a father. I was able to find love in the arms of God, my Heavenly Father. **Galatians 5:1** says, *"Stand fast therefore in the liberty wherewith Christ hath made us free, and be not entangled again with the yoke of bondage."*

In your spiritual growth, you will face many obstacles. You will go through situations you'd rather bury than deal with. However, buried seeds grow roots. In order to stop the spread of unwanted contaminants in your life, you must first discover the lumps before they bring death. **Hebrews 12:1** says, *"let us lay aside every weight, and the sin which doth so easily beset us, and let us run with patience the race that is set before us."*

Once, during a women's conference, the Lord led me to call out several women secretly suffering from various pains and shames. Women began to come forth as God released them from the chains of bondage: abortions, adulterous affairs, unforgiveness, disappointments, and many other things. God forgave these women and healed them of their past.

I pray that you will examine your spirit and be real with yourself. Take the mask off—God can still see underneath it. He wants you whole and not cold. He wants you to experience total peace in Him, not be bound by hidden shame. There *is* life after cancerous lumps.

Chapter Two

~Marred But Not Destroyed~

*A*llow God to shape you into a vessel of honor
according to His purpose for your life through the spiritual
growth process.

We have gone through the broken, bruised, and battered
days of life's dilemmas. There are numerous resources to
help women deal with the pain of being broken. One day,
while preparing for a conference, my mind began to reflect
upon the powerful changes the Master had made in my life. It
was awesome to see that I had gone from being wounded to
being a warrior.

God told me He had chosen me as an anointed vessel for
His glory. It stirs my spirit even now to write about the day
the Lord spoke to me concerning destiny in my belly. I began
reflecting on the pain of my present state, and the bruising of
my past. How could God take such a crumbled past and use it
for His glory? How would He get the glory out of a fallen
vessel, one who had not only fallen, but had fallen badly? To
believe the words God had spoken to me at that time was
seemingly impossible. The Lord was not interested

in dwelling on the things I had gone through—He was more concerned with my destiny: His purpose for my life. I constantly reminded God of all the poisonous lumps He had pulled out of my life. Up until that point in my life, my destiny had been smothered by the pain the enemy had caused, and by the times I had failed the Lord. I did not think I could please God as a broken vessel. I wanted to be able to continue to stand in His presence and to hide behind my mask of pain. The Lord revealed to me that it was not my fear of being used by Him that was keeping me from yielding to Him, but rather, by memories of rejection that had plagued me since childhood. I was afraid that He too would reject me because of the numerous rejections in my past. In the midst of my pain, I wanted God to allow me to continue feeling sorry for myself.

God informed me that His eyes were not focused on what I had been through, but were set on where I was going. Only I was stuck in the past—He had moved on to my future and was trying to pull me there as well. The Spirit of the Lord ministered to me in a powerful way.

And now, the days of crying over the past are gone. I no longer focus on past mistakes and constantly desire the opportunity to make them right. I am no longer wondering and worrying about doors that were closed on me that I felt should have been opened. I am no longer concerned over people shunning me who should have embraced me at times when I needed them the most. God informed me that those days are over. He said, "It happened, now what?"

"The word which came to Jeremiah from the Lord, saying Arise, and go down to the potter's house, and there I will cause thee to hear my words. Then I went down to the potter's house, and, behold he wrought a work on the wheels. and the vessel that he made of clay was marred in the hand of the potter: so he made it again another vessel, as seemed good to the potter to make it. Then the word of the Lord came to me, saying, O house of Israel, cannot I do with you as the potter? saith the Lord. Behold as the clay is in the potters' hand, so are ye in mine hand, O house of Israel."
--Jeremiah 18:1-6

Have you ever seen a sculpture that was the work of a master craftsman? I mean, one that left you speechless, the piece that left no doubt in your mind that the Master took His time during the creation process, and spared no expense during development? Where was such a priceless piece kept during its creation? It had to be concealed until the appropriate time. Could a piece of this magnitude have been created with great ease? It even bore the signature of approval by the master. When the world sees the creator's finished product, thoughts of the creation process may never enter people's minds. They may never be able to imagine the scene of the potter's excitement when the idea for the creation was first conceived. Moreover, who can conceive the frustration of the creator when the clay does not flow through his hands as smoothly as desired because of the rocks, glass, or debris that hinder the process? Despite all hindrances though, the potter does not dismiss the vision of his final creation and cast it away as a fallen idea. Rather than destroy the clay, He takes it and crushes it down to its original form to start all over again.

15

One morning while preparing for work, I picked out my favorite white blouse to wear. Running late, I rushed off to work. Once in the car, I noticed a small spot on the blouse. Hoping that the stain would not be noticeable in the dimly-lit building, I went to work feeling a little uncomfortable about the spot, as there was no time to change. As I walked into the building to start my day, the sun's radiance nearly blinded me. I looked down to avoid the light, and my eyes captured the stain on my blouse. It was more noticeable than I had imagined. The power of sunlight, (son light) is truly amazing. When the Lord shines His light on us, it will immediately reveal any spots or stains we feel are unnoticeable. No matter how well you think they are concealed, or how pretty you shine on one side, the small lumps on the other side always catch His attention.

When a cancerous lump is discovered in a woman's breast, she is advised to have surgery immediately to prevent the spread of the disease. For some women, the removal of the cancerous lump may also mean a mastectomy or removal of the breast, often leaving the woman with deep depression because of the loss. Many of them fear the loss of their attractiveness or social acceptance because of the scars. Too often, the fear of God not finding you attractive enough or good enough to embrace you with His Glory is the same trap the enemy sets for you when God has delivered you. My friend, I denounce the spirit of guilt from your life, now, in the name of Jesus.

When a stain is brought to the potter's attention, he is not distracted because he knows the process of removing the stain. He knows that the power of his skillful hands can mold and shape the vessel as he sifts out the broken pieces and makes the dirt into a master piece. God desires that you mature spiritually to the point where you are aware of your contaminated areas and admit that they are real. He wants you to rise above your pain, knowing that your lumps will not be the determining factor of your destiny. The potter will not present you until He has shaped you to His liking. Many times, however, we seek ways to avoid dealing with issues in our lives that cause us pain. When we do, we allow the situation to lie dormant and to take root in our souls.

God never promised that we would have a trouble-free life. He did promise, however, that we could *"cast our cares upon Him, because he cares for us"* (1 Peter, 5:7). In monitoring our spiritual lives, we must continually do the following:

1. Admit that there is a lump
2. Seek help in the removal of the lump
3. Heal from the wounds of the lump
4. Change our lifestyles for the future

We must thoroughly understand that even upon the discovery of lumps in our clay, the potter does not destroy us. He puts us back on the wheel until the removal process has been completed. We cannot change our past. We cannot change the way we were treated, or the people who mistreated us. We cannot erase the mistakes we've made, or the mistakes of others. We can, however, change our future by accepting the past and learn to heal from the wounds while finding strength in the scars.

I often wonder why I found myself going around in circles with the same situation year after year—different people but the same spirit. The Lord was trying to get me to graduate from this level; however, I continued to fail the test. Tests and trials are not sent by the enemy. In some situations, the Master has noticed a rock or lump in your spirit, and He is forming and pressing you until it is removed. My friend, you will continue to go around and around on the potter's wheel until you allow Him to shape you into a vessel of honor, fit for the Master's use.

Miracle in the Trunk

About three years ago, a friend and I were returning home from an out-of-town meeting. Tired and sleepy, we unexpectedly ran out of gas. The first car we flagged down stopped. After taking a quick glance at the car, my friend suddenly decided walking a few miles would be better after all. However, I was familiar with our location, and I knew that the nearest station was four miles away so we were taking this ride.

When the vehicle approached us, we noticed an elderly couple inside. The car was old, rusty, dirty, stinky, and had holes in the floor. You know, like Fred Flintstone. The couple was dirty, and the smell in the car was awful. I did not want to subject myself to such harsh conditions but I needed help. I asked if they had any equipment to assist us. They both said, "No." Then I asked if they could take us to the nearest station, and they agreed.

Once we opened the door to step into the car, I realized that I had made the biggest mistake of my life. The car was filled with junk and spoiled food that a starving man wouldn't eat. The smell was worst than a burning corpse. The floor of the car on my side had rusted away so I had to hold my legs up to keep from dragging them on the pavement. I wanted to cry, but I needed gas. I wanted to get out, but I needed a ride. I was not sure I could trust these people, but I wanted to get home.

After we got into the car, the man drove about half a mile down the road. He made a statement to his wife that we could not understand, then he turned around. I knew we were going to die, and was preparing myself to fight until the end.

When we made it back to our car, the man pulled his car next to ours. He told us to get out. Then he went to the back of his station wagon and went into the trunk. He began to move things around. He pulled out a nozzle, a gas can, and an old water hose. Next, he began to put gas in our car, and then sent us on our way. Everything we needed was in his trunk. We had judged the car, the man, and his wife based on what we saw, smelled, and felt.

Many times, you may feel you have run out of gas and have gotten off the track. This is the time when God has placed you in position to have faith in Him. God told me that it took faith for us to get in the car, despite what we saw. This is also true when it comes to God using us. He looks beyond all of our faults and sees our needs. He looks pass the dirt, the stinky sin, and the holes that are in our lives and anoints us the more. He has placed everything that we need inside of us (in our trunk). Yes, it takes faith to step out in God. Don't worry when others look at your outward appearance and see old dirt and scars. God is not embarrassed when He anoints us to be vehicles that will carry His word to the next destination. Although we are the vehicles, He is the driver guiding us down the path. The driver is always aware of things He has placed in the trunk for roadside emergencies, as **Philippians 4:19** says, *"But my God shall supply all your need according to His riches in glory by Christ Jesus."*

V.O.I.D.
(Victory Over Inward Dryness)

"Jesus answered and said unto her, Whosoever drinketh of this water shall thirst again. But whosoever drinketh of the water that I shall give him shall never thirst; but the water that I shall give him shall be in him a well of water springing up into everlasting life.The woman saith unto him. Sir, give me this water, that I thirst not, neither come hither to draw."

--John 4: 13-15

When the woman at the well met Jesus, she had a void in her life--something was missing. Though she came to draw natural water, she was in desperate need of spiritual fulfillment.

God desires for us to have total peace within. It is His desire that we walk in total victory in every area of our lives. Many of us are seeking fulfillment in things that feel like the real thing, look like the real thing, and shine like the real thing—but deep in our hearts we know it is only a temporary satisfaction. Some of us have been running on empty for so long that it has become our lifestyle to be unfulfilled.

Jesus was able to fill the inward-dryness of the woman by filling her with a well springing forth with rivers of living water. The woman began to display a level of joy she thought was buried for good. I too, remember the day God filled my spirit with living waters. I was able to smile on the inside, as well as the outside. I could have flashbacks of my past mistakes and not run and hide myself in a shell like a turtle. The thought of God removing the stains and filling me with life was music to my soul.

John 7:38 says: *"He that believeth on me, as the scripture hath said, out of his belly shall flow rivers of living water."* Belly refers to the soul and to the spirit: the seat of the intellect, emotions and desires of man.

When we walk in total victory, believing in Christ, there will be a constant flow of unlimited power to do the work of God as manifested in our lives. In other words, there is going to be a flow out of our belly. It is up to us to have living waters or dead rivers. Either way, there is going to be a flow.

21

When people have a void in their life, they find themselves to be intensely involved in the areas they consider to be their strengths. They are misled to believe that if they receive enough praise, adulation, reward, and stimulation from these areas, they will somehow forget about the void and feelings of emptiness. Others try to escape the silent screams by seeking refuge in ungodly activities, only to realize that they have unlocked the doors to the horrors of hell that take over their lives. In other words, you cannot be delivered from sins or other issues by embracing other sinful acts. It is like telling a second lie to cover the first one you told. Soon, the problem grows beyond recognition. Being busy does not make emptiness go away. Emptiness goes away once the void is filled.

Allow God to fill the void in your life with love and with power by asking Him for eternal water that will fill the secret holes in your life. The word "fill" means to make full, to put or pour into until no more can be received, to satisfy, or to occupy fully. He does not want to satisfy parts of our lives, He wants to satisfy our lives completely.

Remember, in order for God to fill the void in our lives, we must first remove the clog or blockage that is hindering the water from flowing. God can not fill us if we are already filled with contaminated waters.

Although the pain and abuse I suffered at the hands of others seemed unbearable, the damage I had done to myself by living in denial was much worse. God wants to fill every void in your life today— allow Him.

R.E.N.T.
(Redirect Every Negative Threat)

"Casting down imaginations, and every high thing that exalteth itself against the knowledge of God, and bringing into captivity every thought to the obedience of Christ. "

--2 Corinthians 10:5

Once you have allowed God to cleanse your spirit, the stronghold of the enemy is no longer effective in your life. You must be aware of the attacks of the enemy. **1 Peter 5:8** says, *"Be sober, be vigilant; because your adversary the devil, as a roaring lion, walketh about, seeking whom he may devour. "*

My friend, God is going to keep you in all your ways. Give every negative threat the boomerang effect, learning to redirect it with the power of the word of God. Negative comments meant to bring death to my vision, would later fuel my next leap of faith.

There is a divine move of God taking place in the lives of believers. Only those who are not ashamed will be able to say,

"Yes, I had some lumps, but I refused to be consumed and destroyed by unwanted invasions of my spirit. I will go through the process of complete deliverance, and I will allow my circumstances to advance me to the next level in due season, standing as a vessel of honor fit for the Master's use."

Do not allow anyone or anything to disrupt your peace in God. Certainly, the enemy is going to remind you of your past problems, your past mistakes, your past hurts, and even try to show you future dilemmas. It is extremely important that you stay focused. You must begin to "Redirect Every Negative Threat" from your life. When the enemy says you cannot, use the word of God and send every negative threat back. **Philippians 4:13** says, *"I can do all things through Christ which strengthens me."*

I remember secretly battling the spirit of self-doubt after a powerful blow to my self esteem. A prominent professional whom I greatly respected informed me that I had neither the ability, nor resources to attempt my vision, and wouldn't be able to reach the level of people I was attempting to reach. Those words nearly destroyed my spiritual drive and caused me to run out of gas rather than press on. I allowed these words to hinder me for a season. Although my flesh was greatly affected by the negative forecast given to me by this person, I resisted the urge to give up in my spirit. Nonetheless, I struggled to forget those words, as they somehow managed to resurface each time I attempted to move forward. Once a joyful person who loved to share her visions of hope with others, I now refused to share them even with myself. Although my lips said I was not affected by the comments, my actions depicted the truth: the seed of doubt had been planted in my spirit. I soon realized that I had not only allowed those words to hinder me, but had allowed them to completely stop me.

God said, "Whose report are you going to believe, the one who says He has given you power to bring change to the body of Christ, or the one who has no power to give and is in need of help themselves?" I decided to believe the report of the Lord. Although, many negative comments would come and go, I continued to trust the Lord for the provisions for my purpose, and provide He did.

Once you have been set free and begin to obey God, the enemy will attack you with negative words. These potential hindrances may come from those close to you: family, friends, or other loved ones. Nevertheless, you must continue to stand on the word. **Psalms 91:10-11** says, *"There shall no evil befall thee, neither shall any plague come nigh thy dwelling. For he shall give his angels charge over thee, to keep thee in all thy ways."*

A Mirror of Glory

"And we know that all things work together for good to them that love God, to them who are the called according to His purpose. For whom he did foreknow, he also did predestinate to be conformed to the image of his Son, that he might be the firstborn among many brethren. Moreover whom he did predestinate, them he also called: and whom he called, them he also justified: and who he justified, them he also glorified."

--Romans 8:20-28

25

God has called us according to his purpose. Everything in our lives has been predestined to conform us to the image of God for His purpose. Do you know what your purpose is in Christ? In order to walk in the divine call of God for your life, you must commit your will to God. You must become Christ-like in every area of your life, exemplifying God in all you do.

It is the popular thing now to say that you are a Christian. Though these words are very easy to say, the world should be able to look upon a Christian and see the glory of God in him. **2 Corinthians 3:18** says, *"But we all, with open face beholding as in a glass the glory of the Lord, are changed into the same image from glory to glory, even as by the Spirit of the Lord."* One meaning of the word "glory" is majestic beauty; supreme authority or power. "Glorious" means having or deserving glory; famous. "Glorified" means exalted.

In **Exodus 34:30-33**, when Moses had gone up to Mount Sinai in the presence of God to renew the Ten Commandments, it was evident that he had been in the presence of God. He did not have to tell the people because the glory was on his face. We do not have to force others to notice the change in our lives, or to convince them that we have been in the presence of the Lord. The glow of His glory shining on our faces will tell them for us. You cannot hide the glory of God.

We should reflect like mirrors, the glory of the Lord. A mirror displays a virtual image of an object that is standing in front of it; a mirror is something that gives a true picture of something else. God has chosen you, with your past and your weaknesses, for His glory. God wants the world to see Christ in us.

"For ye see your calling, brethren how that not many wise men after the flesh, not many mighty, not many noble, are called: But God hath chosen the foolish things of the world to confound the wise: and God hath chosen the weak things of the world to confound the things which are mighty; And base things of the world, and things which are despised, hath God chosen, yea, and things which are not to bring to nought things that are. That no flesh should glory in his presence."

--1 Corinthians 1:26-29

It may be hard to accept the fact that God would choose someone with your background, your past issues, and your present confusion to change the world. God has chosen the foolish, the weak, the base and the despised things of the world. Why? Simply for His glory. When the world sees that God can use us in spite of where we have been or how messed up we were, He gets the glory. We must seek the Lord for a glory experience. The Bible says in **Romans 8:17-18**,

"And if children, then heirs, heirs of God, and joint-heirs with Christ, if so be that we may suffer with him, that we may be also glorified together. For I reckon that the sufferings of this present time are not worthy to be compared with the glory which shall be revealed in us."

27

I'm Still Here

Go through your situation until the image in the mirror represents what is standing in front of it: His glory.

Let us pray (add your area needs):

Father God, I realize today that I have discovered a lump in my spirit, a lump of depression, abuse, rejection, _____. But Father, today I am going to stay in Your presence until it is removed out of my spirit. I will not allow this to destroy my life or my destiny. It happened, I went through it, and today I'm going to live in spite of it. Father, I leave every unwanted memory in the past. I may have been marred, but I am not destroyed. Though my spirit displays the wounds of my past, the anointing has healed me for the future, and Your power has prepared me for my purpose. I am rising above my pain. Today, I am loosed from every stronghold of my past. I am stepping into a new destiny. Amen.

Chapter Three

~ Provoked to my Purpose ~

*O*ver the past few years we have heard the word purpose more than ever before. Everyone is talking about walking in his or her purpose. I had heard this in almost every service I attended, yet I was not sure what my purpose was, nor did I know if it was time for me to walk in that purpose. I did not have a clue.

I was so excited, motivated, and ready to evangelize the world for Jesus. I was delivered! I began to ask God to show me my purpose for the kingdom. I had no idea what was about to take place in my life. With my new life in Christ, I was ready to obey His command. My excitement soon turned to concern when I began to experience a major attack from the enemy within the body of Christ. I thought, "wait a minute, I am ready to walk in my purpose, not to do battle."

I blamed my church family for allowing the enemy to attack me within the church. I wanted my Pastor to stand up and publicly rebuke the enemy on my behalf. Instead, the enemy was given the glory. Later, I came to understand that through all of that, God was allowing this situation to push me toward my purpose.

My spiritual life began to reflect the life of Hannah in **1 Samuel 1**. Here, Elkanah had two wives, Hannah and Peninnah. Peninnah had several children, while Hannah had no children. **1 Samuel 1:6** says, *"And her adversary also provoked her sore, for to make her fret, because the Lord had shut up her womb."* This story represents one woman appearing to have it all. Peninnah was able to conceive and bring forth much fruit, while Hannah, though she had a husband who loved her dearly, was barren still, and unfruitful.

At one point in my life, I was feeling like Hannah. I had gotten my life together, I knew I was loved and highly favored by the Father, yet I remained barren without a purpose. It seemed that the enemy was producing and reaping the benefits while reminding me of my barrenness. Hanna's desire for purpose was hindered by her depression over her problem. As long as she focused on her problems, her purpose could not come. She went to the temple to pray and began to weep for her blessing.

I too, began to weep and complain about the enemy's taunting. The more Peninnah produced and bore children, the more distant Hannah became. Despite Hanna's plea for a child and the misery of her emptiness, Peninnah continued to provoke her. Perhaps, Peninnah paraded around with her children, attempting to convince Hannah that God could not bless her because she was damaged. This is what the enemy attempts to do with us by reminding us of once-damaged areas of our lives. We must be reminded that we are still in the Master's hands. Damaged goods provide opportunities for the Master to demonstrate his creative abilities in molding miracles.

When I first began to study the book of 1 Samuel, I thought Peninnah was simply an evil woman being used by the enemy to taunt Hannah. **Genesis 50:20** reads, *"But as for you, ye thought evil against me, but God meant it unto good, to bring it to pass, as it is this day, to save much people alive."*

My friend, the pressure of the enemy had provoked Hannah to her purpose. Hannah prayed until her purpose came with power. She conceived and bore Samuel. As for me, I did not know the gift of writing prophetic songs was a part of my purpose until I was provoked by the enemy. I stopped crying over situations in my life, and I got on my face in the presence of God.

I thank God for all the Peninnahs in my life. It was Peninnah who provoked me to seek God's face. God began to sing songs of deliverance in my spirit, songs that would change my life forever, songs that were later recorded and released in 1995 on a CD entitled, *I Will Carry You.*

God wants us to know that He has chosen us for His glory. **John 15 and 16** says, *"Ye hath not chosen me, but have chosen you and ordained you that ye should go and bring forth fruit, and that your fruit should remain; that whatsoever ye shall ask of the Father in my name, he may give it to you."*

I had been praying for my Peninnah to disappear from my life. However, that was not the will of God, for which today I am very grateful. Through my enduring the struggles with Peninnah, a songwriting ministry was birthed in my spirit. I was also provoked to develop a powerful women's fellowship called **Sister Keeper International Ministries**, which also led to the development of a magazine also entitled *Sister Keeper*.

Now, I invite Peninnah to get on my nerves and provoke me. She has been a strong part of my ministry which has pushed me to my purpose. What else can Peninnah pull out of me? Take the stones thrown by the Peninnahs in your life and build a bridge to your destiny. A thrown stone is still a stone which can be used for God's glory. When the bridge is finished, send Peninnah a thank you card and tell her that you appreciate her for the push.

For the bible says, that God will prepare a table for you in the presence of your enemies. When God brings you forth for His glory, it is going to be in the presence of your enemies (Psalms 23:5). Stop praying that your enemies will leave town, find another job, or leave the church. God is going to bless you with them sitting at your table. Today, you should thank God for every Peninnah who was instrumental in provoking you to your purpose.

Look at every positive or negative situation in life as a way to provoke your barren womb into bearing fruit, unlocking the hidden treasures beneath the rivers of destiny.

A Word From An Angel

One morning, I made an appointment with a new hair stylist to get my hair done. When I walked in the shop, I felt very strange. There were no other clients there. *Now ladies, we know that this is not a good sign.* The young woman came out and said that she was ready for me. *Of course she was ready for me—I was the only one there!* I was too embarrassed to leave, but almost too frightened to stay.

When I approached the back of the shop, I noticed an elderly woman sitting under a dryer. After the stylist shampooed my hair, I was on my way to her styling chair, when the elderly lady asked if she could talk with me. "Yes," I said. She told me that she had a word from the Lord for me. Immediately I thought, "not here in a salon!" The lady began to tell me that God said He had allowed everything that I was going through to happen, because He was making and preparing me for a powerful anointing that He had predestined for my life. As she began to speak, the power of God came upon me. She said, she saw brier bushes surrounding me. Just beyond the brier bushes were beautiful gardens filled with different kinds of flowers. Then she said that I was about to walk through the brier bushes, and into the beautiful garden of various flowers. I would have many scars from my walk through the brier bushes, but it would all be worth it, just to sit in the middle of the garden.

I would lose many things in my stormy journey through the brier bush—but one thing was certain: things lost in battle would be regained in victory. By this time, I was wailing before God; however, He would not allow me to go completely out in the spirit until I heard one last thing. Finally, she said God did not want me to be afraid to walk in this anointing. He had chosen me to do a great work for Him, and the beautiful garden of various flowers represented the different lives that would be touched by my ministry. One hour later, I came to myself. I was on the floor of the beauty shop with water everywhere. You see, I never made it to the stylist chair. The stylist was also a Christian, and was running back and forth praising God.

The stylist told me that God had sent me to the shop that morning by divine appointment. She stated that a few minutes before I had arrived at the shop, the phone started ringing with clients canceling their appointments for that day. While I was slain in the spirit, the phone never rang. It was that day that I accepted God's anointing for my life. I thank God for the elderly lady obeying God.

I received another word from an angel who helped heal my soul from the damage caused by the "prominent professional" mentioned in the previous chapter. My older sister invited me to attend a conference at her church. Before service that night, they offered prayer and gave words of prophecy. I had not planned to attend prayer, but only the services. I sat in the sanctuary while my sister went to the room designated for prayer. Finally, she returned and asked me to come back— reluctantly I went.

A young man in the prayer room began to pray for me. I instantly felt the power of God, and knew that this was not just another prayer. The prophet spoke a powerful word in my life that night that changed my way of thinking forever. He began by saying that the enemy had nothing to do with the delays in my ministry that had kept me from walking through a door of opportunity. God had closed the door until my due season. Rather than take me on an elevator to destiny, God had chosen the stairs.

By walking up the steps one by one, I would find the strength and courage to stand in destiny for his glory. He was more interested in my foundation than my roof. Although each step would bring a new challenge, the end would bring new life. Man takes credit for giving opportunities, but God takes credit for creating them. God created an opportunity for my ministry for which no man can take credit.

When God gets ready to speak to you, He may catch you by surprise. Too often we only expect to hear from Him in church during prophetic ministry. However, He may want to speak to you before church, in the grocery store, at the mall, in a park, or even on the job. Be very sensitive to the voice of God. He may come in various forms. Watch for angels sent by Him to comfort your spirit with words of life. My angels had truly delivered me into my destiny.

The Lord later informed me that I was truly a rose in His garden of grace. I was overcome with the glory of His presence as I stood in all humbleness. I began to praise Him for His favor and mercy. Then He challenged me with faith questions:

"can you still be a rose in the desert? Will you shine as an example of hope to those in need of a drink? Will you bloom despite the heat of your surroundings? Will you maintain your color of blood deliverance or will you fade from the radiance of the flaming sun? I began to weep in His presence. God wants us to know who we are in Him and to allow Him to send us forth as examples of hope to others.

Standing Alone In His Presence

The story of the woman brought to Jesus found in the very act of adultery gives us a powerful message of hope. In **John 8: 3-12**, after the woman was caught in adultery, the men took her to Jesus not for salvation, but in hopes that Jesus would condemn her to death. The men's focus was never the woman—it was about Jesus. Their goal was to destroy Christ. The enemy does not want to destroy you—he wants to destroy the Christ in you.

There was no doubt the woman was guilty. Jesus, understanding His purpose, was not about to condemn her to death. For He was sent to save those who are lost, not destroy them. Jesus exercised wisdom in healing the woman who was probably broken, embarrassed, and ashamed. Although the men brought her to be stoned, they brought her to the right place. When the ordeal was over, the men left, and the woman was standing alone in the presence of Jesus. I find this to be awesome! Many times it may appear to the enemy that you are at the place of death; but to God, it is a place of life, healing, deliverance, restoration, joy, peace, and happiness. The enemy pushes us to our death only for us to find life.

Are there situations in your life that have found you guilty? Do you feel these situations have pushed you to condemnation? Think about it: the best place to be pushed, is alone in the presence of Jesus. The word "alone" simply means apart from others. It is when we are alone and still that God can speak to us. God wants to put us in a place where we will be able to hear only Him.

Let's give God a praise:

Father I thank you because:
My pain led me to prayer
My making came through my breaking
My birthing came through my bruising
My deliverance came through my death
My power came through my praise
And my problems provoked me to my purpose

Chapter Four

I Will Live Because I Shall

There I was participating in a worship service where praise was lifted from my lips like the sounds of angels—my adoration to God was a prolific touch of my eternal gratefulness while tears of intense emotions fell as His presence filled the room. It was at that moment that I felt the scripture ring so true in my spirit: *"I can do all things through Christ which strengthens me."*

Months earlier, I had gone through one of the greatest challenges in my life: an attack against my ministry. Surrounded by those who encouraged me, I attempted to press forward, convincing myself that I would not allow anything to hinder my destiny. However, when my friends went home and the lights went out, I quietly admitted to myself that the vision appeared dead, without possibility of resurrection.

"Rejoice not against me, o mine enemy when I fall, I shall arise; when I sit in darkness the Lord shall be a light unto me." **-- Micah 7:8**

I began to fake happiness in the presence of others while secretly experiencing the battle of overcoming dead issues. I had allowed my vision to die based on the predictions of others. The previous days, once filled with the anticipation of new discoveries of destiny, became filled with present memories of shattered dreams linked to broken promises. However, after reading **Ezekiel 37**, the resurrection of new life was breathed into my soul as I declared, "I Will Live Because I Shall!"

I was presented with the decision to choose life or death for my destiny. I was asked, "can your bones live again? Can you push past your problems and into your purpose? Are you fearing the future by focusing on the frustration of the fight?" I responded with the words, "I will live again." The Lord replied that my "will to live," was not enough; He said to me, "you must move past your *will* to live and into your *promise of life.*" The word "will" means a desire, and "desire" is a will to do something. The word "will" also means the power to decide or control what one will do or how one will act. I had more than a desire for life. God had given me a promise of life.

Ezekiel 37:14 is a promise from God for new life which says, *"And shall put my spirit in you, and ye shall live, and I shall place you in your own land; then shall ye know that I the Lord have spoken it and performed it, saith the Lord."* I embraced the will to live, by standing on the promise of "I Shall." The word "shall" means am, going to, destined, certain, compelled, and must. Now put "I" in front of the meaning of shall. This allows the meaning to come to life. There was no way I or my vision could die. I had His spirit in me, and was destined to live.

40

The prophet Ezekiel was instructed to prophesy unto the bones until they received life. True life to me represents, Living In Full Evidence of the power of God. **John 10:10** says, *"Christ came that we may have life and life more abundantly. The thief cometh not, but for to steal, and to kill, and to destroy: I am come that they might have life, and they might have it more abundantly."* The enemy had come to kill, steal, and destroy my vision. I no longer wanted to pretend with my friends or lie to myself. I wanted real joy, real peace, true worship, and the abundance of life.

Can you remember what God has spoken about your life? Have you been waiting for years for the vision God promised concerning your life to come forth? Do you feel that your vision has come and gone and you missed it, or perhaps that it is too late for your vision to be manifested? Does it appear too late to hope or that it is too impossible to believe that after everything you have experienced in your life, you can still live in victory according to the word of God?

The reality of life for many Christians today is merely survival. The world is surviving. God has given the Christian more than the ability to survive. Anyone can press through dilemmas, survive, and still be filled with bitterness from the painful struggle. I am talking about Christians *living.* Many have allowed their situations to force them into survival, while they have secretly refused to live.

What determines whether or not a person breathes in the breath of life, or inhales the toxins of death?

41

Ezekiel 37:9 says, *"then said he unto me prophesy unto the wind, prophesy, son of man, and say to the wind, Thus saith the Lord God; Come from the four winds, O breath, and breathe upon these slain, that they may live."* The bones were slain. In other words, they were there because something or someone had killed them. There are four types of slain visions among Christians today:

1) **Murder:** Those who fell into traps of the enemy disguised as people eagerly wanting to help them reach their purpose, only to find out too late that they were collaborating with the enemy. Those who allowed the words of others and the attacks of the enemy to kill them by destroying them with their tongue. There is life and death in the power of the tongue (Proverbs 18:21).

2) **Suicide:** Those who decided to destroy their own visions due to the final judgment and words of others. Constantly hearing others referring to you as "she use to be anointed." Those who took their vision and destroyed it with their own mouth, their own hands, and own disbelief because of the pressure and attacks of the enemy. Many also destroy their visions because of past or present mistakes. Remember, God does forgive, just ask Him (Luke 11:4).

3) **Natural Causes:** Those who got tired of waiting on their visions to come to pass. Giving up, feeling they were too old to produce in their old age. **Ezekiel 37:11** says Israel referred to themselves as bones that were dried up, bones with no hope, and bones that had been cut off. This slain individual waited on their visions to come to pass for so long that they forgot what the vision was, and simply gave up.

4) **Coma**: These are the saints who continue to come to church but have no life in them. They must have artificial breath to cause them to move. They continue to lay in their beds of death, out of touch with reality, refusing to fight through the traumas of temporary defeat. Individuals floating in pride that refuse to admit they have gotten off track from the purpose and plan God has instructed for their lives. They refuse to come back to reality and start over.

"The Lord is not slack concerning his promise, as some men count slackness" (2 Peter 3:9). God waited until Abraham was old and passed his days of performing, and until Sarah's womb had died, before he spoke life to their promise. Sometimes God will wait until your vision appears dead to you and those around you to breathe life into dead, broken dreams, and shattered visions. What hinders you from having your vision full of life?

I Speak Life In You

Is your vision dead? Have you smelled the stench of rotten flesh and seen maggots cover your vision, dreams, family, church, job, or even yourself? Has there been a death you neglected to notice? You may not have seen the tombstones or even viewed the body, but you have noticed someone missing. Is it you? You must admit that for whatever reason, your vision is dead, or appears that way.

No matter how long your vision has been dead, how many others do not believe you have heard from God, or how many times you have attempted and failed, you must be able to press forward and flow in the purpose God has for your life.

43

God is constantly saying, "can these bones live?" Having a vision without life is like having your spouse tell you that he or she loves you, without illustrating it through actions. Stop dragging around a corpse that once housed your dreams. Allow the Lord to breathe life into your vision. Do not wait until you hear the applause of the people before you raise the curtains. Burn the obituaries filled with the accomplishments of your past. Cancel the flowers filled with the aroma of death. Silence the choir singing the songs of doom.

The portrayal of the children of Israel in Ezekiel 37 as dry bones scattered in a valley of unfulfilled purpose is a profound passage of scripture often observed time and time again in the body of Christ. God asked Ezekiel an astounding question: "can these bones live? Today the question is being asked of you: "can your vision live?"

God commanded the prophet to instruct the bones to hear the word of the Lord. If we are going to live, we too must hear and apply the word to our lives. What is the word for our dry situations? We are not truly living if we are not walking in the evidence of what His word says about a life filled with Christ. God wants you to live out your vision exemplifying the power that He has put inside of you for His glory.

Remember, God told the prophet to tell the dry bones to hear the word of the Lord. Let us look at the Word and see how we "SHALL" live. Throughout the scriptures, God uses the word "shall" to reflect the power and authority given to us as believers. We must first understand power and authority.

Power is the ability to act or to do, while authority is the right to command or to act; it is the power to enforce obedience. God has given us the right and the ability to live life to the fullest. Too often, we spend countless hours in prayer asking God to do something He has already given us the power and authority to perform. It is not that God does not hear our prayer—He is simply waiting on us to exercise with power, the ability He has given us, and the authority to command change in our environments. He wants our lives to be a reflection of the applied word, and our prayer lives to be filled with hearts of thanksgiving.

There are seven principles of SHALL from the scriptures that we are going to address. Indeed, there are more principles; however, we will examine seven, as it represents the number of completion. Each time you read the word SHALL, replace it with the following meanings: I am; I am going to; I am compelled to; I am destined to; I am certain to; and I must.

The Seven Principals of SHALL:

1. **Shall by Purpose: John 14:12** says, *"Verily, verily I say unto you, He that believeth on me, the works that I do SHALL (must) he do also, and greater works than these SHALL (must) he do, because I go unto the father."*

2. **Shall by Promise: Matthew 6:33** says, *"But seek ye first the kingdom of God and his righteousness and all these things SHALL (are certain to) be added unto you."*

3. **Shall by Power: Luke 10:19** says, *"Behold I give unto you power to tread upon serpents and scorpions, and over all the power of the enemy, and nothing SHALL (must not) by any means hurt you."*

4. **Shall by Prayer**: **Matthew 21:22** says, *"And all things, whatsoever you SHALL (will) ask in prayer, believing, ye SHALL (are destined to) receive."*

5. **Shall by Performance: Mark 16:16-18** says,
   "He that believeth and is baptized SHALL (is destined to) be saved: but he that believeth not shall be damned. And these signs SHALL (are certain to) follow them that believe, In my name they SHALL (must) cast out devils, they SHALL (compelled) speak with new tongues. They SHALL (are going to) take up serpents and if they drink any deadly thing it SHALL (will) not hurt them, they SHALL (are going to) lay hands on the sick and they SHALL (must) recover."

In addition, **Matthew 18:18** says, *"Verily I say unto you, Whatsoever ye SHALL (must) bind on earth SHALL (is certain to) be bound in heaven and whatsoever ye SHALL (must) loose on earth SHALL (is destined to) be loosed in heaven."*

6. **Shall by an Out-Pouring: John 7:38** says, *"He that believeth on me, as the scripture hath said, out of his belly SHALL (must) flow rivers of living water."*

7. Shall by Prophecy: Acts 2:17-18 says,

"And it Shall (is destined to) come to pass in the last days, saith God, I will pour out of my Spirit upon all flesh; and your sons and your daughters SHALL (are compelled to) prophesy and your young men SHALL (must) see visions and your old men SHALL (going to) dream dreams. And on my servants and on my handmaids I will pour out in those days of my Spirit and they SHALL (are certain to) prophesy."

I began to prophesy the Word to my vision by standing on the promises of "I shall." The word "shall" to me became an awesome demonstration of the power of God when I realized it represented to Suddenly **Have ALL**. I found myself worshiping God out of a spirit of true life. Even when the music had ended and my friends were gone, there was still peace and new life in my belly. What an awesome feeling!

When you walk under the anointing of "SHALL," you are not frustrated by what you see or do not see. You do not waste time defending or even tracking down lies. Even when the vision seems dead, you rejoice, knowing that death cannot cause your "SHALL" to cease. Problems cannot stop your vision, and people leaving cannot hinder you. Those knowing the power of "shall" simply obey and wait on the evidence of a predestined promise of their "SHALL" to come forth.

If you will begin to live your life in the power and authority of God, walking under the anointing of "I SHALL," your life will be changed forever. Keep a journal of all the things that

47

God has promised for your life. My life has not been the same since the Lord gave me this revelation of the word "SHALL."

Do not settle for a vision filled with brittle bones, contaminated by the residue of rotten flesh. Use the word of God as you embrace the promise of, "I Will Live Because I Shall." Allow the word of God to speak life to your vision until He shakes your broken promises into powerful purpose, and until He mends your disrupted dreams into divine destiny.

Choose Life

The Lord told the prophet Ezekiel to prophesy to the dry bones. The man of God had to speak the words of life. We too must speak the words of life by calling those things that be not as though they were. (Romans 4:17). Once you have been released from your grave clothes, you must begin to prophecy your destiny into existence. **Proverbs 18:21** says, *"Life and death are in the power of the tongue."*

Prophesy means the foretelling of the future. What is your choice today? Are you going to live or your going to die? Prophesy the word to your situation, your circumstances, and your environments.

The choice is yours. In **1 Samuel 17**, when David was preparing to defeat the Philistine, he was so assured of his victory that he prophesied to Goliath concerning the outcome. David gave Goliath a list of things that would take place on the day of his defeat. Saul offered David his armor to wear, but David had enough wisdom to know that you can not win a battle walking in someone else's anointing. David chose to use the things God had anointed him to use. He was a shepherd anointed to protect the sheep. What has God anointed you with? It may seem small and insignificant to others, but for you it means life. Use what God has given you to defeat the giants in your life.

David used spiritual things to prophesy his victory: his faith, his power, and his actions. He also used natural things to prophesy his victory: a shepherd's bag which contained rocks to protect the sheep in times of trouble, smooth stones, and his sling. We should at all times, be equipped, prepared and ready to demonstrate the gifts of God. David was armed with things which were familiar to him. In our lives, our Bible should represent the shepherd's bag, which we can reach into at any given time. Our smooth stones are to represent the Word of God, in which we are able to pull out a scripture of promise at any given time. Our sling is represented by our mouths, speaking forth words of life from God. David took the head off of the enemy. We have been tearing at the body and the smaller parts of our problems. Let us take down our giants at the head.

Recently, while ministering at a women's fellowship using a message entitled "I Will Live Because I Shall," the Lord told me to look out the window. He asked me what I saw." "Cars," I said. Yet, I knew that was not what He was after from me. He then instructed me to look again. This time I noticed several trees. I saw two tall trees swaying with full, beautiful, green leaves in the middle of several smaller trees. The smaller trees stood motionless with dry brittle limbs and had the look of death. He then said, "how is it that trees in the same area, receiving the same light, being nourished with the same rain can reflect such different outcomes?" Tears began to roll down my face as I understood so clearly what He was saying to me. What made the trees different? The green trees had chosen life, and the dry, brittle trees had chosen death.

This is so true of us today. The same words of life are offered to all of us by the same Father, through the same Holy Spirit. Yet, those who choose life will live in the fullness of life, while those who choose death will remain in a life of limited ability. Friend, I speak life in you. I speak life to your spirit. I speak life to your dreams, to your mind, to your situations, and to your family. Choose LIFE, **L**iving **I**n **F**ull **E**vidence of His power. God wants you to live a Christian life projecting His glory to the highest in every area of your life. God has given you the right to your vision and the ability to command the vision to come forth. You shall live and not die. With Christ you SHALL (**S**uddenly **H**ave **ALL**).

With this revelation, we must stand in the truth declaring, "we do not have to pray another prayer, sing another song, or fast another day for the power of the anointing of God to flow in our lives." When we received the Holy Spirit, He gave us all the power we needed to defeat the enemy and to walk in victory. Now that we have heard the Word, and have believed the Word, we can finally act upon the Word. On the other hand, praying, singing, and fasting will develop a closer intimacy with God. The church is waiting on God to rain down a new anointing filled with supernatural power.

However, God is saying, "I am waiting on the church to walk in the fullness of the power and the authority that I declared before the beginning of time."

He is waiting on us to rise up and declare that we are not going to take it anymore. We will not stand by and watch our children kill children, or allow our children to fall into the destructive pits set by the enemy. We will no longer allow our churches to continue praising God as worshipers in a graveyard. We will not allow our leaders to oversee us, being double agents living secret lives. The enemy is not destroying our nation; the church is. When we do not walk in the authority God has given to us to speak life and command change, we sit by and become pallbearers for the enemy.

God gave me the words to the following song which brought LIFE (**L**iving **I**n **F**ull **E**vidence of His Power) to my vision and deliverance to my soul.

"I Speak Life in You" (song released 2000)

Though it seems like you have failed
and though it seems like you are losing the fight in all
of your trying.
Don't let nothing turn you around, for the end is near
and we're preparing to meet the King.
So pull down every stronghold, rise and stand for God is in
control.
I break the hold and destroy every fear
He's got a plan for you , and you can go through
I break the hold and destroy your fear,
He's counting on you and you can go through.
Just stand on my promise
and stand on my words
I speak Life in You
Yes, there is Life in You.
Because you are a winner
You are a fighter
I made you a warrior
and You are more than a conqueror.
I speak life in you!

Chapter Five

~ *G. R. A. C. E.* ~

God Releasing Anointing To Change Environments

$\mathcal{I}$ looked on my porch one day and saw a bird sitting on the corner ledge. I assumed he was there to rest for a moment from his tiresome journey. However, four months later the bird was still there. He would come each afternoon around 5:30 p.m. and leave each morning around 6:00 a.m. One morning while driving to work, the Lord spoke to me and said, "look at the bird." I knew instantly that God was trying to reveal something to me. I had constantly questioned Him concerning the fact that the bird had chosen to camp out at our house.

God asked me if I knew why the bird was there. I said, "No." I had not invited him, nor had I placed food out for him. However, because of the length of time he had stayed with us,

"For my grace is sufficient for thee: for my strength is made perfect in weakness. Most gladly therefore I would rather glory in my infirmities that the power of Christ may rest upon me."

--2 Corinthians 12:9

I bought him a bird house and asked my husband to put it up for him. The bird did not like us tampering with the area that he had already prepared for himself. When we installed the bird house, the bird moved to the other end of the porch.

God explained to me that the bird represented His grace in our lives. We had not invited it, nor had we done anything to deserve it. His grace just shows up in our lives. God does not need us to tamper with His grace in order for it to abide in our lives. He only wants us to receive His grace, to stand in awe of its presence, and to act in obedience to His command. From that day forward, I embraced a new meaning of God's "GRACE:" (God Releasing Anointing to Change Environments).

Finally, after God had revealed the significance of such a powerful illustration, the bird we referred to as Grace flew away. Our lives had been changed forever in the way that we understood God's grace. I knew that Grace had flown to her destiny. I began to praise God for allowing me to have such an awesome demonstration of His love towards me.

Five months later, while watching the news, I heard the news reporter issue a warning concerning Hurricane George which was heading toward our region. There were possible threats of destruction to our area. The storm had already killed hundreds of people and destroyed the homes of many others. I began to pray. I began to prepare my home for the approaching storm. As I went to secure the front door, the Lord led me to open the door. I looked on the porch, and to my surprise, sitting on the corner ledge was Grace. I asked the Lord why Grace had come back. The Lord then asked me,

"what is about to take place in your city?" "A storm," I
answered. I was about to learn more about God's grace.

The Lord revealed to me that the storm heading towards
our city had the same potential for causing severe damage and
disruption to our lives the same way the enemy does when he
attacks us. During the times of storm in our lives, many will
begin scurrying around like mice caught off guard by a cat's
presence. As Christians, we must understand that the grace of
God will show up in our lives long before the storms to
anchor us with the power to stand during the windy turbu-
lence. When the enemy shows up, he will find you fully
protected by the grace of God.

Well, Hurricane George came and went—and when the
storm was over, Grace was still sitting on the porch. God is
an awesome God. God wanted me to be assured that in the
next level of anointing, when the storms come and go, when
situations rise and fall, I would stand knowing that I was
standing in His grace.

After each powerful move of God in my ministry, His
symbol of grace has appeared in my life. Grace, our bird, has
continued to show up many times at my home. Many people
have come to view this powerful, symbolic expression from
God. It is a reminder that His grace, His love, and His mercy
is also present. One night, after a powerful service, despite
the enemy's attack, I returned home to find two birds nestled
on my porch. I felt God as He smiled on me that night; I
continued to acknowledge the presence of His grace in my
life. I soon began coming home from ministering, expecting
Grace to meet me there.

Today, I am continuously asked, "when was the last time you saw Grace?" Now, I am expecting to see Grace make an appearance symbolic of new destiny upon the completion of this book. It is only by His grace!

Revival recently broke out in our church, with people as young as three years old being slain in the spirit of God. I returned home after service, basking in the glory of God. Around 12:30 a.m., while reading, I stopped to thank God for His presence in the service. I was so excited about what He was doing, that I expressed to Him, that in times like these, Grace routinely shows up to reflect Your approval. The Lord then instructed me to go outside; if I wanted to see Grace, she would come. I then told Him it was June; I did not think she would be there at all. He said to me, "Go." I retrieved my glasses and ran to the front door feeling somewhat silly. I opened the front door expecting to see Grace sitting on the ledge of the front porch. Unfortunately, she was not there. I closed the door and returned to bed. Immediately, the Lord spoke to me and said, "Go look again." I looked again, and at the other end of the porch, sat a powerful move of God's promise to us. It was a reminder that this revival had happened because of His grace and simply for His glory.

Stand

"For now we live, if ye stand fast in the Lord."
--1 Thessalonians 3:8

After a powerfully-anointed service, where the glory of God was revealed in a way that I had never seen before, the Lord also spoke to me in a way that I shall never forget.

There was a young girl about thirteen years old visiting our church for the first time. During the service, the Lord led her to give to me a powerful prophecy about going to the next level in my destiny. This was extremely important for me to hear. You see, during the previous few weeks, I had been praying and seeking God for direction and for timing about the next step in my destiny. God had instructed me to go into full-time ministry, and of course, I had some reservations. I would often feel that I was not prepared or ready for this challenge. Yet, I would obey the Lord.

As I was slain in the spirit, the Lord instructed me to open my eyes. My eyes locked onto the sound speaker which rested on a tripod stand. He first directed my eyes to focus on the tripod stand. I found this very strange, but I kept looking. As my eyes continued to lock in on the stand, the awesome words of revelation began to come forth. I noticed that the stand had three base legs which were connected to a leg in the center. The three base legs were stabilized on the floor, while the center leg was hovering in the air. The center leg was prevented from touching the floor by the strength of the three base legs. The Lord then instructed me to notice the giant speaker which sat on top of the single leg in the center. It was then that I heard my Heavenly Father say to me,

"daughter, it is not your strength that is going to allow you to step into the next level of anointing; it will be Mine. Just as all three base legs are connected to the center pole, I want to connect you to the Father, the Son, and the Holy Ghost. Think it not strange that I have chosen a tripod stand to illustrate this message to you. For as long as you stay connected to me,

I will never allow you to fall, but to STAND. The call of anointing for ministry may seem too heavy on your single pole, but the sound that is going to come out of you will be magnified with each level as the dial is turned and the anointing is stirred up in you."

Although I knew the Lord was my strength, I thanked Him for taking something as simple as a tripod stand to demonstrate His love, His strength, and His commitment to never forsake me or let me fall so long as I stayed connected to the Father, Son, and Holy Ghost. I told my Heavenly Father that night that I was ready to carry the sound of deliverance for His glory because my soul was anchored in Him, and my foundation was stable.

When the service was over, still basking in His glory, I attempted to drive home. As I approached my street, my eyes focused on a truck in front of me. I heard the Lord say to me, "look at the truck." I looked at the back of the truck. There in the corner of it, God had a final message for me that night. The message said, "WHERE WILL YOU GO NEXT?" Amidst my crying, I said, "to the next level."

We must truly realize that God will not allow us to fall. He wants us to walk in obedience to the plans and the purposes that He has laid out for our lives. You can never fall as long as you are connected to the Father, the Son, and the Holy Ghost who make it possible for you to STAND.

Why me? You say, I did no harm
I just wanted to stay, safe in His arms
But every time I would make it there
Something would snatch me back, before I was aware
Alone you think....Where do you go next?

To look back now would be outrageous
Having gone through all the stages
Times were hard and long
The enemy fought you, I mean fought strong
And now the question is ...Where do you go next?

The tears flowed, the heart ached
Time and time again, you had to be fake
Yes you laughed and yes you smiled
In a state of shame in a state of denial
Confused you wonder...Where do you go next?

Now after all, what is the goal
To live in love, to redeem your soul
Am I to rejoice, and live without lack
Am I to walk forward and not look back
Trying to figure out...Where do you go next?

And then one day, it all became clear
You're the head not the tail, there is no fear
You have the victory, you have already won.
God is your Father, He sacrificed His Son.
Now your basking in His Glory...Where do you go next?

Then your spirit quickens, as the anointing flows
You are covered by the blood, and the Holy Ghost
You see clearly now, it was all just a test.
Preparing you for a peaceful rest.
You're feeling wonderful.... But....Where do you go next?

You are the chosen people, you have been set apart
You live for His Glory, after His own heart
In a place of Worship, is where you stay
On you face you enter, In His presence you lay.
You have it all together, Now it is all clear...
So you thought...

Then the question arises... Where do you go next, IN HIM?

By Tammy Whiten

Where do you go next?

Chapter Six

~ *I'm Still Here* ~

I hear a song in my spirit which says, "I've been through the storm and the rain, but I made it. I've had sickness and pain . . . oh . . . I made it. I spent many nights alone, seemed like all my hope was gone, but hallelujah, thank you Jesus . . . I made it." What a powerful song! And yet, many stay focused on the words, "I've been through the storm and the rain," rather than, "but I made it".

Take a deep breath and exhale a sigh of relief. Just the title of this chapter should make you shout. By now, you should be getting your praise on. It does not matter what you have gone through to get to this point. The fact is, "you are still here." Did you really believe when you were down on the floor in your bedroom begging God to take your life, screaming that you could not take it another day, that you would ever see today? Think about it. If the enemy had known that attacking your body with sickness would cause you to develop an even greater level of faith, he would have left you alone. If he had known that being abused, mistreated, and lied on would

And we know that all things work together for good to them that love God, to them who are the called according to His purpose.

Romans 8:28

have made you this anointed, he would have forced truth to be your best friend..

If he had known causing you to lose your job, and the security it gave, would cause you to start your own company, offering you more stability, he would have given you a raise and a promotion. If the enemy had known that being rejected by family, friends, and other loved ones would drive you into the arms of the Master, he never would have messed with you in the first place.

This chapter serves the enemy notice that despite the disappointments, failures, mistakes, abuse, and shame, you made it to your destiny anyway. He may have robbed you of some things during the voyage, or caused you to leave some things behind; however, he could not drive you crazy, take your life, joy, or peace. What he meant for bad, has really been for your good. The word has already declared that we SHALL live and not die.

In **Acts 16:16-34**, Paul and Silas demonstrate a powerful lesson of going through a dilemma with praise. They were faced with what the enemy thought was a tremendous problem.

While walking in their purpose, they were thrown into prison. Today, we call it emotional bondage. The enemy thought this would stop their mission. They were stripped of their clothing, beaten, publicly shamed, shackled, and thrown into prison. Sound familiar? Far too often this is the description of an anointed vessel. The enemy believes if he can hinder you enough, beat you down enough, strip you of some friends, loved ones, and things, lock up some potential blessings for a season, or put enough pressure on you by shackling your feet to remind you of previous bondage each time you attempt to get free, that you will somehow give up and quit.

Paul and Silas demonstrated seven "P" attitudes, (again, the number of completion) that we can use to walk in total victory to our destiny:

1) Go through a problem
2) Exercise power
3) Faith in God's promises
4) Give God praise
5) Demonstrate peace
6) Walk in our purpose
7) Stand and proclaim victory.

First, we must go through the problem. Walking in your purpose will provoke the enemy to hinder you by sending the spirits of fear, discouragement, and intimidation. You must go through the problem in order to reap the rewards of the struggle. You must continue to pull down every stronghold of the enemy. Always remember that the battle is not yours; it is the Lord's. He will always make a way of escape for His people. Stand still and watch God open doors where there are none.

Paul and Silas required no prompts from the lesson "I SHALL" when they exercised power to cast the spirit of divination out of the damsel on their journey. They knew they had power over the enemy. Although the damsel praised and acknowledged them as servants of the most high God, they recognized that her words were false flattery, and demonic situation, neither were they distracted about what the enemy viewed as a temporary setback, God was going to use their setback for a permanent promotion. Paul no doubt remembered the promise of God's word to him at the beginning of his destiny tour in Acts 9:15. It was revealed in him that he was a "Chosen vessel for the glory of God." You also must stand on the promise God has spoken to you concerning your life.

Even though Paul and Silas were physically locked up in prison, their spirits were free to praise. We also must learn to praise God in spite of it all, even in the midst of our adversities. Although they were in prison together, the Bible does not tell us whether or not Paul and Silas were in the same prison cell. The only thing that we know for certain is that they were in the same prison for the same reason. Matthew 18:20 declares that where two or three are gather together in God's name, He is there in the midst of them. The enemy messed up when he put Paul and Silas in the same situation, at the same time, serving the same God.

Paul and Silas agreed to stand and praise God because they knew that there was victory in praise. When we give true praise to God in our situations, the foundations will be shaken to the very roots of the problem. All doors will be opened and every locked situation will be released. When we praise God, we SHALL (are destined to) cause others to be set free. I dare you to find someone who is going through what you are going through and have a praise party instead of a pity party. God will be in your midst.

A word of warning to people of purpose: be very careful when confiding in others while you are under pressure. Your fellowship should be with those who exemplify the same anointing as yourself. It should also be with people who encourage you, ones who build you up, or stir up the call of God in your life, and genuinely want to see you succeed.

Psalms 133:1 declares, *"Behold how good and how pleasant it is for brethren to dwell together in unity."* The key word is unity.

Through the beating, stripping, and even the pain of being shackled, Paul and Silas continued to demonstrate peace. No matter what happens to you, you must not allow your problems to disrupt your peace. **Isaiah 26:3** says, *"I will keep you in perfect peace whose mind is stayed on thee."* The enemy will magnify the pressure of your problems expecting you to panic and to lose control. Can you remember a time when you thought the enemy had stolen or robbed you of a promised miracle? You know, the things God showed you in a deep, long winter's dream while on vacation in the mountains. The things God promised He had prepared for you alone, only to awaken and to discover that the enemy had disrupted your dream and sabotaged your miracle. Do not allow the enemy to disrupt your dreams of destiny by thinking and speaking foolish words of death such as, "that was supposed to be for me," or "my breakthrough will never come." What God has for you, is for you. Remember, your strength lies in your praise. Despite what Paul and Silas had endured in the darkness, they continued to sing and praise God throughout the night. Tell your situations: "no matter how bad it gets, even if I have to cry, I am still going to praise the Lord all through the night."

While sitting at home one afternoon, I began to wonder why I had experienced some of the awful things that had occurred in my life. Little did I know that God would send a powerful word to me later that day through my armourbearer, Tammy. She called and stated she had a word from the Lord for me. She had taken the word and placed it in a frame as a constant reminder of His promise. When I opened the package and looked in the frame, in that moment, God immediately answered my question. It read, "I had to go through what I went through, to go through what I am going through." The Lord said, "think it not strange the path you have taken. For it may have caused pain in your life for a season, out of the results will bring freedom to the lives of others for an eternity."

What was the purpose of Paul and Silas going through this dilemma? God will use your situations to cause others to be totally set free. I like to refer to this as being "locked up to loose." Now, that is a powerful message. I will preach that one day. There are many situations that you may have experienced which have nothing to do with you and all to do with the person next to you. Paul and Silas praised God not only until their chains were loosed, but until the chains of those they were sent to minister to were also broken. This proves that they were "locked up to loose." Have you been placed in a situation of discomfort to bring deliverance to someone else? Will their chains of bondage be broken when they hear the anointing in your praise?

Finally, when the night was over and morning had come, the keeper returned to the prison and found the prison doors opened. Seeing the doors opened, he thought the prisoners had escaped. That is when Paul stood up and made one of the greatest proclamations ever given, "we are all here." The word "proclaim" means to announce, and to announce means to give a public notice; to give notice of the arrival or presence of. Paul gave the public announcement of freedom and gave notice of the presence of God. He proclaimed to the keeper, that although the midnight experience of praise had freed everyone from the chains of bondage, they were STILL there. The word still means even after that; in spite of what has happened; and nevertheless. In other words, after all we have gone through, and in spite of all that has happened, we did not run away. We were beaten, stripped and locked up publicly before our enemies; and now we have remained here to publicly show the enemy the miracle of the "suddenly" experience God gave us at midnight. That is powerful!

While writing this chapter of the book, I caught the end of a movie late one night. A young woman had been stalked by a crazed killer who eventually vowed that he would take her life. One night, the attacker attempted to carry out his plan. The young woman awoke the next morning in the hospital. At her side was her crying daughter. She asked her mother what had happened to her, and what the crazed killer had done.

The woman had been beaten, raped, and stabbed. Her face had been pounded beyond recognition. She looked her daughter in the eyes and told her it did not matter what he had done to her, and did not matter what she had endured the night before, because she had awakened to see another day. She was still here.

Can you think about a time the enemy tried to take you and your family out? Now, think about how you felt when the enemy came back expecting to find you dead, but instead, found you alive and praising God. Someone in need of a healing should let the doctor know that I have come back to show you that, "I am healed, I am not dead, and I am still here." Somebody needs to return to the divorce counselor and tell them "he did not leave me—we are both still here."

Whatever your situation is, I dare you to declare that after all you have been through, you are still here. You are here in your right mind, did not go crazy, and are not out on the street. You are still here with a powerful ministry, and a better family than before. You did not leave the church, and are still here praising God.

It's Morning Time

When morning comes for your life, it is proof that the hand of God is upon you. While Paul and Silas were going through their dilemma, the keeper referred to them as prisoners. When morning came, he could see the glory of God on them. He then referred to them as "Sirs," fell down and declared he would serve the Lord. They were made to suffer throughout the night; but as the Word of God says, *"weeping may endure for a night, but joy comes in the morning"* (Psalms 30:5).

My friend, you must never attempt to demand the respect of others. Allow God to do that for you. People may not respect the anointing on your life while you are going through, but hang in there, your morning shall come. They may have called you an unqualified, unanointed, broken, and a rejected vessel with a crushed vision; but, when it's all over, they will see that despite what you have been through, you are still here with a divine purpose.

The keeper of the jail was instructed by the magistrates to escort Paul and Silas out of the city through the back exit; however, Paul refused to leave quietly. Paul declared since they had been accused, beaten, stripped, and locked up publicly, they would also be released publicly.

When God has brought miracles of deliverance in your life, do not allow the enemy to send you away quietly after he has attempted to destroy your life publicly. The enemy allowed you to go through sickness publicly; you nearly lost your mind publicly; your husband left publicly; you lost your job publicly; you were lied on publicly; and you were even brought in the presence of your enemies publicly. And now that God has brought restoration to you and your family, you should proclaim your testimony of praise publicly. Face your enemy and declare,

"I know you did not expect me to make it through, but somewhere between midnight and morning, God sent an earthquake and shook my life and the lives of those around me. So no, I am not going to be quiet. I will shout it on the rooftop. You thought you had destroyed me for the last time when you left me shackled by heavy burdens beneath the load of guilt and shame, in the dark horrors of a cold cell filled with sin's stains. I began to praise God from the depths of my soul, and that is when He touched me and made me whole."

I am reminded of the three Hebrew boys, Shadrach, Meshach, and Abednego, who were thrown into the fiery furnace. I am sure the king thought he would return later to bury their scorched bodies. But God! When the king returned, he found the three Hebrew boys proclaiming, "we are still here, you threw us in the fiery furnace, you turned the heat up seven times hotter, (again, the number of completion), you kept us here until you thought we were completely dead, but even in the midst of the fire, God gave us the strength to stand."

By now, if you have read this far, you should be ready to explode in your spirit. This chapter is for those of you who know where you are going in Christ, and for those of you who have sold out to God and were not a sellout. You know you are anointed, and that the call of God is on your life. You understand that because of the anointing, it is inevitable that you will face opposition. This book is for the individuals who will stand on the promises of God, no matter what . . . no matter what is thrown at them; no matter what they have to go through; when it's all over, they are still a winner. No matter what lies you have sent my way, or how many doors have been closed, when the dust settles, I am still going to be here with a praise.

Focus on the reason God allowed you to go through all that has happened in your life. Why are you still here? Is it to cry over wounds that you refuse to let heal? Or did you go through to evolve into a warrior willing to win? I dare you to prophesy to yourself. Despite all that has happened in your life, you are still here. You may have been abused or left alone. You may have committed many sins that are too painful at times to even think about. You may have failed God many other times in your life. But today! I dare you to lay this book down for a moment and reach down into the depths of your soul and declare, "I did not go crazy; through it all, I am still anointed. My husband, friends, and family may have left me alone, but I am not alone. Even though I thought I wouldn't make it through it all, I am still here." Say it again: "I'm still here!"

Chapter Seven

~ It's My Turn Now ~

My Due Season

*I*f you have made it to "due season" in your life, your ministry, or your purpose, then this is the time when all the pieces of the puzzles of life somehow come together. At this point, the revelation of **Romans 8:28**, *"And we know that all things work together for good to them that love God, to them who are called according the His purpose,"* has begun to be revealed to you.

What does it mean to step out in your due season? Let us take a look at the meaning of "due" and "season." Due means to arrive in time; scheduled; appointed; or the expected season. Season refers to a period in which a special time of harvest or type of agricultural work is carried on. Combine the meaning of these two words in the spirit, and we can easily understand that there are no late seasons in God.

"And let us not be weary in well doing, for in due season we shall reap, if we faint not."

--Galatians 6:9

It is extremely important that you understand God's timing for your life. He has a set time for you to step out into your destiny. However, despite the fact of knowing their time of destiny is already set, many refuse to wait on God.

Have you ever bought fruit out of it's season? If you have, there were probably several things you immediately noticed concerning your fruit:

(1) It was not as sweet as it is when you buy it in season

(2) The color is not as clear because it has not gone through the full developmental stage

(3) The smell is not a normal, sweet aroma

(4) Fruit will cost you triple out of season. Getting out of God's timing will cause you to become bitter when things do not work out for you as you had expected. It will cause you to fade away quickly because you went without a developed foundation on which to stand. It will give you an imitation flavor that will not be pleasing to those in your presence.

(5) Finally, going forth out of your season will certainly cost you more than waiting on your scheduled time of arrival. Time is the period or the moment when something occurs; the customary, fixed, or appointed moment; or the hour for something to happen. Waiting on God requires less effort, and thereby produces better fruit

Stepping out into your purpose without God's endorsement is like buying a ticket for a movie that has not yet been made. You need to see the previews first before the movie can be rated. God has been in the process of making you into an award-winning vessel. He is about to unveil you to the world. Let the Master take pride in unveiling the vessel that He has spent countless days and years molding into His image. Friend, your season of deliverance is already fixed, so wait.

Expectant mothers are often asked, "when is your baby due?" In other words, "what is the expected time of arrival? Babies often come earlier than the projected date; and some arrive later than projected. Unfortunately, some mothers get tired of carrying the weight of pregnancy and its discomfort. In an attempt to cause the baby's early arrival, some even resort to artificially-induced labor.

Many have discovered that these attempts can be deadly to themselves, and to their unborn child. As a result, some have even died, simply because they could not wait for an inevitable due date. Do not destroy your destiny simply because you can not wait. Whether babies arrive earlier or later than man's projected date, they are still on time with God.

You must also stand strong while you are waiting on God. **Isaiah 40:29-31** says, *"He giveth power to the faint but they that wait upon the Lord shall renew their strength they shall mount up with wings like an eagle, they shall walk and not faint, they shall run and not be weary."*

For many years, I understood this scripture to mean that if you wait on the Lord, He would renew your strength only after you have made it through the storm and reaped your blessings and promises. You would then be able to run and not be weary, walk and not faint after you had made it through. This made perfect sense to me. It is very easy to get excited and praise God when the blessings come. However, this passage should display our actions during our time of waiting. I now understand it to mean, while I am waiting on God to move in my situation, while I am waiting on my season to come, and while I am still going through, He gives me strength to mount up with eagle's wings, the strength to continue to soar through the storm, the strength to run through heated times and not get tired or give up, the strength to walk through the valley of the shadow of death and still not faint.

You must continue to wait on the Lord in every area of your life. Do not become weary and decide to proceed in your purpose without His approval. Do not allow yourself to become faint and simply quit during your time of preparation. Weary means to become tired of doing what you know is right to do. When we become faint, we start doubting, fearing, exercising unbelief, and experiencing discouragement.

Sometimes God will show you a vision concerning your life; however, it may be ten, fifteen, or twenty years before it comes to pass. "What about words of prophecy?" you may ask. You must be extremely prayerful when you receive a word of prophecy concerning a move of God in your life. I do not want you to believe that I am against personal prophecies because I am not. The gift of prophecy is one of the strongest gifts of the spirit operating in my ministry. Because of the anointing, I feel that it is imperative you understand why God allows a word of prophecy, or a word of inspiration to be spoken into your life.

Prophecy comes to confirm what God is doing or going to do in your life. It does not always manifest immediately. For example, I have seen people receive a word of prophecy concerning a time of marriage approaching, and as a result, marry the first man who comes along. Even after a word of prophecy, you must always consult God and wait on His timing. You must wait on God.

There were many things spoken in my life through words of prophecy long before I accepted the call to ministry. Some were even received while my life was in shambles. Yes, while I was broken and battered, God sent countless words of prophecy that I would someday minister to broken, battered, and bruised women who would become warriors in worship.

One day I asked the Lord why He had allowed many men and women of God to speak such powerful words into my life at times when my entire life was in a broken state. The Lord allowed me to understand that in my state of weakness, He never saw me as a broken vessel. He saw me as the vessel He had preordained me to be: a vessel of honor. He only saw me for what He had created me to be, not for who I was at that moment. Although I had to go through a period of brokenness and pain, He knew that my time of destiny was set, that my due season would surely come, and that my time of preparation would mend the broken pieces, and remove all the stains.

In **1 Samuel 16,** David was anointed king, but not because he had made the right connections with man. He did not have to pay for the king's seat by planting the biggest seed into Samuel's ministry (you know, those who plant seeds to be seen, hoping to be chosen to minister at the next conference). David did not mail out an elaborate resume, filled with altered truths and prudent lies, hoping to get noticed.

When Samuel came to anoint the next king, David was not even invited to the selection ceremony. David was out in the field fulfilling his responsibility. God is calling forth individuals in this hour of due season who are waiting on their next promotion by working faithfully at their current level of responsibility. God is calling you forth because you are already faithful.

Have you sometimes felt that while others were being voted MVP (Most Valuable Player), you were being selected as the LLS (Least Likely to Succeed), and about to be cut from the team? Perhaps David's family had already counted him out as being king because they never asked him to come forth for the selection process. Do not worry when you are not invited to the selection ceremony being conducted by man.

It is not the invitation of man you are waiting for in the mail. You are waiting for a personal invitation from God concerning your next promotion.

David did not look like a king, nor did he act like one. He was more concerned with protecting his sheep. He had already proven his commitment to protecting them by killing a bear and a lion trying to harm them. Later, he proved his strength by killing a giant.

God is looking for someone who knows their call, has gone through the process, and is ready to come forth. Even if lions, bears, and giants get in the way of what God has said, those who have been through the process will destroy the enemy, in the name of Jesus, and continue to magnify God. God is looking for bear-slayers, lion-destroyers, and giant-killers.

It was David's appointed time to become king. Nothing could stop that from happening. Even if he was not invited, God held up the ceremony until David arrived. Nothing can hinder your time of arrival in God either. There is no need to fall into the traps of humanistic tactics that many others have tried. God does not send your season any sooner because you prayed all night, fasted all year, nor gave 20% tithe. God is a God of timing.

There was a set time for the Savior to come to give His life for us; there was a set time for Him to die; and there is a set time for His return. Now, get this into your spirit: there is a set time for you also. Wait on God; He will bring you forth in your due season.

Receiving Miracles from Good Ground

Mark 4:20 refers to the people of God as being "good ground" when they hear the word, receive the word, and bring forth fruit. I have often wondered why God used the term "good ground."

One day while preparing for a message, the Lord began to unfold the understanding of this parable to me and the significance of Christians being called good ground. The parable in Mark chapter 4 makes reference to four types of soil:

1) **The wayside**: those who hear the word but refuse to obey it.

2) **Stony places:** those who gladly receive the word, but have no root to stand when trouble comes.

3) **Thorns:** those caught up on material blessings rather than the blesser.

4) **Good Ground:** those who hear the word, receive the word, and bring forth fruit.

Let's focus on good ground for a moment. For years, we have been functioning at the level of hearing and receiving the Word. It is now time to operate in the level of bringing forth fruit. This is for the individuals who have heard the word, received the word down into their spirit, obeyed the word, and are now ready to present fruits of miracles from good ground. Many of us cannot reap miracles from our soil because we have not allowed God to develop our ground into rich soil. In order to better understand the significance of being made good ground, we are going to look at the five changes that soil goes through during the developmental or preparation process, and how it relates to Christians being referred to as good ground.

1) Changes in partial size: This process occurs when the rocks and the minerals are broken by physical and chemical forces. Some of the forces used in this process are wind and water (rain). Christians experience a partial breaking when we allow God to force unwanted issues out of our lives. It is in our developmental process that God wants to break up the mountains that can hinder our growth: various weights, sins, unresolved forgiveness, and other issues in our lives. This is the process of the potter removing the lumps.

2) Organic matter: In this process, dead things are added to the soil to provide nutrients. What are the dead things that God adds to our soil to provide the spiritual nutrients of life? When we allow the areas in our lives that are not pleasing to God to completely die, the death of those situations provide the needed nutrients of life for a future full of hope. Unfortunately, many of us attempt to destroy the demons in our lives by displaying a history of wounds. God is not moved by the wounds of your flesh or by your situations. He is only moved by the death of them.

3) Leaching: This process involves the movement of materials into place. At this stage, the soil is beginning to form. During this process, God may have to move or shift some people around in your life, in order to mold you into the image of Christ. He does this to prepare you to become good soil. Do not panic when friends no longer want to be around you. It could be God putting you into position to seek His face. Sometimes, even your best friend may hinder you from hearing from God. There are times when God may have to let you get fired in order for you to be moved into position to start your own company. Everything may seem crazy in your life right now, but rejoice. It could be God moving you into position for a miracle.

4) Eluviation: During this process, the materials are moved into suspension. Suspension means to keep from falling or sinking through the force of gravity. Think about this powerful action. You will be placed in a position in God where the enemy's attacks cannot cause you to fall. That is powerful! In other words, by the time you get to the fourth stage of development, it does not matter how bad things appear, you cannot fall. No matter how strong the enemy pulls, his forces will not cause you to sink under pressure. Can you feel the hand of God moving you into position? The whirlwinds of spiritual change have come to suspend your purpose into position. Once God has moved you into position to stand, the forces of gravity cannot pull you down. According to **Jude 24**, *"Now unto him that is able to keep you from falling, and to present you faultless before the presence of his glory with exceeding joy."*

5) Illuviation: When materials are deposited into the soil. It is during this stage of development that God gives words of direction for your destiny. Once God has cultivated your life to withstand any climate, He is then ready to deposit His seed of the anointing into your life. Sometimes the hardest ground to cultivate brings forth the greatest flow of fruit. Your hardest situations can produce visions of life. When Joseph was thrown into the pit by his brothers, what appeared to be his end resulted in a young man being put in position to go from his problems to his purpose. While Joseph was in the pit, a place of darkness and loneliness, the path of purpose was revealed, which unfolded into a bridge to destiny.

If God has to till your soil over and over again until it becomes purified, He will. If He has to let the sun shine until it burns every infected area out of your life, He will. If He has to allow the wind to blow until you give up your will and run to him, He will. If He has to stand guard all night to ward off intruders until the morning comes, He will. Once you are ready to bring forth fruit of miracles from the soil God has created in you, He is going to deposit His anointing upon your life so that you may stand boldly for His glory.

You must allow God to prepare your soil to endure the hot, scorching summer, and the long, bitter cold of winter. Allow Him to keep you from falling in the fall, while giving you strength to spring forth in the spring. God has planted the seed, cultivated it, carried it, watered it, and now has the roots firmly planted. I think I can see some fruit on your tree.

God wants you to bring forth fruit for His glory. The Master Farmer wants to see the results of His time of investment. As you were once contaminated dirt that has now been cultivated into rich soil by His hands you will produce fruit in due season, and will bring Him all glory. It is then that you receive miracles of LIFE (Living In Full Evidence of His power) from your soil. You can truly walk in the power of "I SHALL," because "it's your turn now," as your due season has finally come.

It Was Worth It All

Nothing compares to the moment of delivery. The atmosphere is filled with the excitement of the arrival of new life. No thought is given to the prior months of pain and anguish— and all eyes are focused on the unveiling of a miracle. It is during your time of delivery that it becomes obvious to you why you had to go through such an extensive preparation process.

Esther 2:15 says, *"Now when the turn of Esther, the daughter of Abihail the uncle of Mordecai who had taken her for his daughter was come to go in unto the king, she required nothing."*

In the search for a new queen, Esther enters the contest under the advice of her uncle, Mordecai. Here, Esther demonstrates the greatest example of walking in your call when it is your turn. Esther, along with others vowing to become the next queen, was sent through the one-year preparation process. Although it was predestined that Esther would become the next queen to bring deliverance to her people, it was imperative that she complete the cleansing process. She had to wait on her time of invitation. Your destiny does not exempt you from time of preparation.

After all the contestants had gone through the preparation process, they saw the king individually. Esther stood back and allowed everyone else to parade their talents and gifts in front of the king.

Today's Esthers are watching others attend conferences in hopes of being noticed, making connections with the right people, planting seeds of abundance for attention, and spending needed finances on publications, in hopes of learning the secret of being presented, while she patiently waits her turn.

Do not become frustrated in waiting on your turn to be presented before the king. You do not have to become restless while others are being presented before you. Don't become fretful and think someone else is going to skip you in line. Do not get caught up on foolish tactics to be noticed. God does not need your help opening a door, nor does He need you to seek out others to unlock doors, when He knows He is the only one with the key to your destiny.

The Bible says that your gift will make room for you, not you make room for your gift. You must understand that the contest is fixed. The winner was chosen before the pageant started. Once again, remember that the race is fixed, but the next queen cannot be announced until she is ready. Until you have gone through all the levels of your promotion, there will not be a crowning of the queen. It is time for your crowning.

Having the right people of God in your life during your time of presentation is extremely important. Esther did not become Queen because she knew it was her turn. She entered the pageant because Mordica knew it was her turn. Esther was surrounded by people sent into her life by God who believed, perceived, prepared, protected, and pushed her to her purpose. Listen to those God has sent in your life for guidance and instruction.

Always remember that your push into destiny is not just for you. You represent those who taught you, led you, worked with you, and prayed for you. It is now time for you to do the same for the people whom you have been called to minister unto.

Your turn in destiny does not mean that others in your surroundings are not anointed. The women being presented to the king had all gone through the same process of preparation and cleansing. Remember, going through the preparation process is the first step. Waiting on your season is the next.

When it is your turn, no one can tamper with the ballots. While others perform with gifts and talents, all will step aside and stare in awe as you gracefully enter the stage.

What has God prepared you for? Can you rise up today and declare, "after all I have been through I am still here with a praise?" If you are still here, then why are you? Could it be that God has brought you this far to deliver your destiny? The hardest time of delivery is right before birth. Proclaim today that it is your turn now to accept the invitation from the king.

Remember, you require nothing but the favor of God; He has prepared you well. There is a powerful anointing being released upon your life that is going to bring glory back to the church, change in our communities, harmony in our homes, safety in our schools, and power in our praise. Has God called you to bring deliverance to your people for such a time as this?

Forget about your broken past. Now it's your turn to step on stage. Nothing can stop your purpose. It's your season--so push today until you deliver.

The invitation has been sent and received.
You must R.S.V.P. immediately please.
The audience is awaiting to see the unveiling
of a masterpiece,
that will be used to bring deliverance to all they meet.
The Master Creator is admiring the work of His hands,
it all turned out the way He planned.
He started with clay, filled with lumps; but
He never once doubted what the clay would become.
Although it took years to develop and create,
every tear was worth it for this moment today.
He's not worried about His creation falling at all,
for He sealed your destiny long before you were called.
Your name has been called and your time appointed,
you mustn't worry you're also anointed.

I'm Still Here

Remember as you enter, the presence of the King,
give Him thanks and praise for everything.
Others attempted to please Him somehow,
but you SHALL succeed because IT'S YOUR TURN NOW.
The trials and problems, that came to destroy and kill,
have all been broken because YOU ARE STILL HERE.
The curtains are rising, and your name has been called.
Can you see His Glory?
Your pain and suffering has been worth it ALL.

The Sister Keeper Vision

Behold how good and how pleasant it is for brethen (sisters) to dwell in unity. Colossians 3:15

Sister Keeper is a non-denominational, multi-cultural, non-profit, Christian women's fellowship with a vision of providing support, encouragement, and ministry opportunities to women. Sister Keepers goal is to support women with established ministries as well as encouraging and training women to actively seek their purpose or role in the body of Christ.

The ministry is also setup to empower women with the opportunity to release their purpose by networking with other women ministries through fellowships, conferences, and the Sister Keeper quarterly magazine.

1. **Quarterly Fellowships** *(every three months) in various cities and states with the focus on building unity, speaking life, deliverance and restoration with an anointing that will bring a life changing experience.*
2. **Intercessory Prayer** *in a group or alone every Wednesday, praying for leaders, women and families.*
3. **Unity Networking** *through Sister Keeper Quarterly Magazine*
4. **Community light** *–actively participating in community functions to assist in special needs including food, clothing, job training, etc.*
5. **Annual Women's Conference** *– Held in September. Bringing established ministries together in Unity.*

The Sister Keeper Magazine

In today's time God is raising up a people who are after his own heart. So many women have tapped into their destiny and are now walking by faith.

There are women from all walks of life who have testimonies and visions that need to be shared with the body of Christ. Thus the vision and purpose of the Sister Keeper Magazine is to give these women the opportunity to do just that. The magazine has become a major source of sharing situations, determinations, and destinations both nationally and internationally. The women in the Sister Keeper Magazines are truly anointed blessed women of God.

The Sister Keeper magazine is a full color magazine, with powerful testimonies, inspirational writings and conference advertisements among other wonderful inserts.

If you know of someone you would like to see featured in the Sister Keeper Magazine, please email us or call us, we will be more than happy to review your suggestions.

P.O. Box 15597-Pensacola, FL 32514 or
Sisterkeeper@aol.com or 1-866-439-1410

Sister Keeper Quarterly Magazine
1 year Subscription $20 or $3.50 an issue plus $2.50 Shipping.